100%
Vegetarian

FUN FOOD FOR CHILDREN

TARLA DALAL
India's # 1 cookery author

S&C

SANJAY & CO.
BOMBAY

CREDITS

First Printing 1999
Copyright © Sanjay & Company
ISBN No. 81-86469-33-8

Price : **Rs. 95/-**

Published & Distributed by
SANJAY & COMPANY,
353/A-1, Shah & Nahar Industrial Estate,
Dhanraj Mill Compound, Lower Parel (W), Mumbai-400 013.
Tel: (91-22) 496 8068. Fax: (91-22) 496 5876.
Email: books@tarladalal.com

Research & Production Design	Designed by	Photography
PINKY CHANDAN	S. KISHOR	VINAY MAHIDHAR
ARATI KAMAT		
JYOTI SHROFF		**Food Styling**
		NITIN TANDON

Printed by JUPITER PRINTS, Mumbai.

OTHER BOOKS BY TARLA DALAL

INDIAN COOKING
→ Tava Cooking
→ Rotis & Subzis
→ Desi Khana
→ The Complete Gujarati Cook Book

WESTERN COOKING
→ Eggless Desserts
→ Mocktails & Snacks
→ Soups & Salads
→ Mexican Cooking
→ Easy Gourmet Cooking

HEALTH COOKING
→ Low Calorie Healthy Cooking
→ Eat Your Way To Good Health

GENERAL COOKING
→ Exciting Vegetarian Cooking
→ Party Cooking
→ Microwave Cooking
→ Quick & Easy Vegetarian Cooking
→ Saatvik Khana
→ Mixer Cook Book
→ Pleasures of Vegetarian Cooking
→ Delights of Vegetarian Cooking
→ Joys of Vegetarian Cooking
→ Cooking with Kids

EASTERN COOKING
→ Chinese Cooking
→ Thai Cooking

MINI SERIES
→ A New World of Idlis & Dosas
→ Cooking under 10 Minutes
→ Pizzas and Pasta

INTRODUCTION

No more boring breakfasts, soggy tiffin boxes and unhealthy snacks for your children.

Healthy food makes your child's body and mind healthier, so your child will have more energy to enjoy learning and playing!

Here's a book created just for you! It is full of easy to follow recipes that are fun to make as well as scrumptious to eat. It has been designed and developed to help all busy mothers cater to their children's fussy food habits.

This book helps you plan delicious treats for your children at all times of the day. It includes an array of recipes for breakfast, school time munchies, after school treats, sweets and delicious drinks.

Have fun cooking these recipes for your children and watch their faces light up as they enjoy them! Happy cooking.

Tarla Dalal

INDEX

POWER POHA

A simple breakfast preparation made of poha and kabuli chana.

⇩

Preparation time: 10 minutes.
Cooking time: 20 minutes.
Serves 4.

⇩

2 cups poha (beaten rice)
1/3 cup kabuli chana (chick peas)
1 onion, chopped
1 green chilli, chopped
1 tomato, chopped
2 teaspoons lemon juice
1 tablespoon oil
salt to taste

For the garnish
2 tablespoons chopped coriander

1. Wash and soak the kabuli chana for about 6 hours.
2. Pressure cook the kabuli chana. Drain and keep aside.
3. Heat the oil in a saucepan. Add the onion and green chilli and sauté till the onion turns translucent.
4. Add the tomato and cook for a further 2 minutes.
5. Add the kabuli chana, lemon juice and salt and mix well. Remove from the fire.
6. Sprinkle some water on the poha to moisten it and add it to the kabuli chana mixture.
7. Mix well and garnish with the coriander. Serve hot.

BROKEN WHEAT UPMA

A broken wheat variation of the traditional semolina upma.

⇩

Preparation time: 15 minutes.
Cooking time: 20 minutes.
Serves 4.

⇩

½ cup broken wheat (bulgur)
1 onion, chopped
1 green chilli, chopped
¼ cup green peas
¼ cup carrots, diced
1 tablespoon oil
salt to taste

⇩

For the garnish
2 tablespoons chopped coriander

1. Clean and wash the broken wheat thoroughly. Blanch it in 2 cups of hot water for 4 minutes. Drain and keep aside.
2. Heat the oil in a pressure cooker. Add the onion and green chilli and sauté till the onion turns translucent.
3. Add the peas, carrots, broken wheat and salt and sauté for 3 to 4 minutes.
4. Add 1½ cups of water and pressure cook for 1 whistle.
5. Garnish with the coriander and serve hot.

- **You can use any other vegetables of your choice.**
- **Bulgur wheat or broken wheat is also called "Cracked Wheat" and is available at any grocer.**

****

YUMMY APPLE PORRIDGE

A wholesome porridge cooked with apples.

⇩

Preparation time: 5 minutes.
Cooking time: 10 minutes.
Serves 4.

⇩

¼ cup broken wheat (bulgur)
¼ cup quick rolled oats
1 cup milk
½ cup sugar
1 apple, diced
2 tablespoons butter

1. Clean, wash and drain the broken wheat.
2. Heat the butter in a pressure cooker and sauté the broken wheat in it for 3 to 4 minutes.
3. Add the oats and cook for a further 2 minutes.
4. Add the milk and 1 cup of water and pressure cook for 2 whistles.
5. Add the sugar and apple pieces while the porridge is hot. Mix well.
   Serve warm or chilled.

- **You can use jaggery instead of sugar for this recipe.**

****

QUICK RAWA AND VEGETABLE DHOKLAS

A nutritious version of the traditional Gujarati recipe.

⇩

Preparation time: 10 minutes.
Cooking time: 10 minutes.
Serves 3 to 4.

⇩

1¼ cups semolina (rawa)
2 cups buttermilk
¼ cup boiled vegetables (carrots, french beans, corn etc.),
finely chopped
2 teaspoons ginger-green chilli paste
1½ teaspoons Eno's fruit salt
1 tablespoon oil
salt to taste
oil for greasing

⇩

For the tempering
1 teaspoon mustard seeds (rai)
1 teaspoon sesame seeds (til)
a pinch asafoetida (hing)
1 tablespoon oil

1. Mix the semolina, buttermilk, vegetables, ginger-green chilli paste, oil and salt in a bowl to make a smooth batter. Keep aside for at least 30 minutes.
2. Add the fruit salt, mix well and pour the batter into a greased 200 mm. (8") diameter thali. Steam for 8 to 10 minutes.

3. Prepare the tempering by heating the oil, adding the mustard seeds, sesame seeds and asafoetida and frying until the seeds crackle. Pour the tempering over the prepared dhokla.
4. Cut into pieces and serve hot with green chutney.

Variation:
QUICK VEGETABLE IDLIS. You can also steam the batter to make idlis.

● **It is important to add the fruit salt just before you put the dhoklas to steam and to ensure the water is boiling when you put the dhoklas to steam.**

****

PROTEIN PARATHAS

Picture on page 17
⇩
Parathas made of paneer and spring onions, packed with the goodness of whole wheat.
⇩
Preparation time: 10 minutes.
Cooking time: 15 minutes.
Makes 6 parathas.
⇩
½ cup paneer, grated
2 spring onions, finely chopped
¾ cup whole wheat flour (gehun ka atta)
2 green chillies, finely chopped
salt and pepper to taste
⇩
Other ingredients
oil to cook

11

1. Combine all the ingredients and knead into a soft dough using water.
2. Divide into 6 equal parts.
3. Roll out each portion into a circle of 125 mm. (5") diameter.
4. Cook each paratha on a griddle (tava), smearing a little oil, until both sides are golden brown.
   Serve hot with Sweet and Sour Tomato Relish, page 79.

Serving Suggestion:
Banana Yoghurt Shake page 77 is the perfect accompaniment for Protein Parathas.

Variation:
You can also make JALEBI PARATHAS as shown in the picture on page 17.

● **You can also use spinach or carrots instead of the spring onions.**

****

BANANA WALNUT PANCAKES

Delicious breakfast pancakes.

Preparation time: 10 minutes.
Cooking time: 10 minutes.
Makes 8 pancakes.
⇩
1 cup plain flour (maida)
2 ripe bananas, mashed
¼ cup walnuts, finely chopped

12

¾ cup milk
4 tablespoons castor sugar
½ teaspoon vanilla essence
¾ teaspoon baking powder
1 tablespoon melted butter
⇩

Other ingredients
butter to cook
honey or jam to serve

1. Combine all the ingredients in a bowl and mix well to make a smooth batter, making sure that no lumps remain. Keep aside.
2. Heat a non-stick pan, spread about 3 to 4 tablespoons (¼ cup) of the batter to make a thick pancake of about 100 mm. (4") diameter.
3. Cook the pancake over medium heat, using a little butter to cook both sides until golden brown.
4. Repeat the same for the remaining batter to make about 8 pancakes.
   Serve hot with honey or jam.

● **Use over-ripe bananas for best results.**

* *

POWER PACKED CEREAL

Picture on page 17
⇩

Makes an excellent high carbohydrate breakfast for kids.
⇩

Preparation time: 5 minutes.
Cooking time: 30 minutes.
Makes approx. 450 grams.
⇩

2 cups rolled oats
¼ cup sunflower seeds (optional)
1 tablespoon sesame seeds
½ cup wheat germ or cornflakes
½ cup brown sugar
½ cup mixed chopped nuts (cashewnuts, walnuts, almonds)
3 tablespoons vegetable oil
¼ teaspoon vanilla essence
¼ teaspoon salt
2 tablespoons raisins

1. Mix the oats, sunflower seeds, sesame seeds, wheat germ, brown sugar and chopped nuts in a bowl.
2. Mix the oil, 1/4 cup of water, vanilla essence and salt and whisk together. Add to the above dry ingredients.
3. Spread the mixture in a baking tray and bake at 160°C (320°F) for 20 to 30 minutes, turning occasionally, until crisp and golden. Cool.
4. Add the raisins and store in an air-tight container. Serve with milk and fruits.

****

PITA POCKETS

Picture on page 18
⇩
Nutritious whole wheat pita breads cooked within minutes on a griddle.
⇩
Preparation time: 20 minutes.
Cooking time: 15 minutes.
Makes 8.
⇩

For the pita bread
1 cup whole wheat flour (gehun ka atta)
1 teaspoon (5 grams) fresh yeast, crumbled
1 teaspoon sugar
1 tablespoon oil
½ teaspoon salt
⇩

For the dressing
3 tablespoons fresh curds
2 spring onions, chopped
1 clove garlic, chopped
¼ teaspoon cumin seed (jeera) powder
½ green chilli, chopped
salt to taste
⇩
1 recipe nutritious patties, page 20
⇩

Other ingredients
2 tomatoes, thinly sliced
1 cup lettuce, shredded

15

For the pita bread

1. Combine all the ingredients except the oil in a bowl and knead into a soft dough using enough water until it is smooth and elastic.
2. Add the oil and knead again.
3. Cover the dough with a wet muslin cloth and allow it prove till it doubles in volume (approx. 15 to 20 minutes).
4. Press the dough lightly to remove the air.
5. Divide the dough into 4 equal parts.
6. Roll out each portion into a circle of 125 mm. (5") diameter and 3 mm. (1/8") thickness.
7. Cook the pita breads on a hot tava or griddle on each side for a minute or until the bread puffs up.
8. Remove and keep aside.
9. Cut each pita bread into 2 halves.

For the dressing

Blend all the ingredients in a food processor to get a smooth sauce. Keep aside.

Top Right: Power Packed Cereal; *page 14*
Center: Protein Parathas; *page 11*
Bottom left: Sweet and Sour Tomato Relish; *page 79*

How to proceed

1. Warm the pita bread halves on a griddle (tava).
2. Fill each pita bread half with the tomato and lettuce, one Nutritious Patty and a tablespoon of the dressing on top.
3. Repeat for the remaining pita bread halves and other ingredients to make 3 more Pita Pockets.
   Serve immediately.

- **You can also serve the pita pockets with red garlic chutney.**
- **Use any other patties or cutlets of your choice for filling the pita pocket.**
- **You can use 1/2 teaspoon (2.5 grams) of dry yeast instead of the fresh yeast for the above recipe.**

****

Top Right: Orange Raisin Muffins; *page 67*
Bottom Left: Pita Pockets; *page 15,* filled with Nutritious Patties; *page 20*

NUTRITIOUS PATTIES

Picture on page 18
⇩

Broken wheat, vegetables and paneer make a mouth-watering combination for a patty.

⇩

Preparation time: 10 minutes.
Cooking time: 15 minutes.
Makes 8 patties.

⇩

¼ cup broken wheat (bulgur)
1 carrot, grated
1 onion, finely chopped
¹/₃ cup mushrooms, finely chopped
½ cup paneer, grated
1 tablespoon soya sauce
1 tablespoon chilli sauce
2 tablespoons whole wheat flour (gehun ka atta)
salt and pepper to taste

⇩

Other ingredients
oil or butter for cooking

1. Clean and wash the broken wheat thoroughly. Blanch it in 1 cup of hot water for 4 minutes. Keep aside.
2. Combine all the ingredients in a bowl and mix well.
3. Divide the mixture into 8 equal parts and shape into patties.
4. Shallow fry the patties using a little oil on a non-stick tava, cooking on both sides till golden brown in colour. Serve hot with ketchup or chutney.

● **These patties also make a great filling for burgers.**

****

CHEESY NOODLE VEGETABLE CUTLETS

A snack that can be made in minutes.

⇩

Preparation time: 10 minutes.
Cooking time: 15 minutes.
Makes 12 cutlets.

⇩

1½ cups cooked instant noodles
½ cup sweet corn kernels, cooked and crushed
2 green chillies, finely chopped
2 spring onions, finely chopped
3 tablespoons tomato ketchup
½ cup grated cheese
½ cup dried bread crumbs
salt and pepper to taste

⇩

Other ingredients
dried bread crumbs for coating
oil to shallow fry

1. In a bowl, combine the noodles, sweet corn, green chillies, spring onions, ketchup, cheese, bread crumbs, salt and pepper and mix well using your hands.
2. Divide the mixture into 12 equal portions and shape into cutlets .
3. Coat the cutlets with dried bread crumbs and shallow fry in oil on both sides till golden brown.
   Serve hot with ketchup or green chutney.

****

DELICIOUS SANDWICHES

Picture on page 36
⇩

Apples and carrots make a delicious sandwich combination.
⇩

Preparation time: 5 minutes.
No cooking.
Makes 3 sandwiches.

⇩

9 bread slices
⇩

To be mixed for the Apple spread
1 apple, grated
1 tablespoon cheese spread
salt and pepper to taste
⇩

To be mixed for the Carrot spread
3/4 cup grated carrot
2 tablespoons cheese spread
salt and pepper to taste

1. Apply the apple spread on one bread slice. Sandwich with another slice of bread.
2. Spread a layer of the carrot spread and sandwich with a third slice of bread.
3. Repeat to make 2 more sandwiches.
4. Remove the crusts and cut into 4 triangles.

● **These are great for lunch box meals.**

****

CHATPATA CHAAT

Picture on page 54
⇩
Jhatpat to make and chatpata to taste.
⇩
Preparation time: 5 minutes.
Cooking time: 5 minutes.
Serves 4.
⇩
2 cups mixed sprouts, boiled
¼ cup sweet corn kernels, cooked
2 spring onions, chopped
¼ cup tomatoes, chopped
1 teaspoon chaat masala
1 recipe sweet chutney, page 81
salt to taste
⇩

For the garnish
sev
coriander leaves
papdi (sevpuri), crushed

1. Mix all the ingredients in a bowl.
2. Garnish with sev, coriander leaves and crushed papdi.

****

GREEN PEAS
SANDWICHES

Colourful sandwiches filled with tomato and crushed green peas bound in a cheesy dressing.

⇩

Preparation time: 5 minutes.
Cooking time: 10 minutes.
Makes 4 sandwiches.

⇩

8 bread slices
1 large tomato, thinly sliced

⇩

To be mixed into a filling
1 cup green peas, boiled and crushed
1 tablespoon celery, finely chopped
2 tablespoons eggless mayonnaise, page 84
1 tablespoon cheese spread
salt to taste

1. Toast the bread slices.
2. Arrange the tomato slices on a toasted bread slice.
3. Top with the filling and cover with another slice of toasted bread to make a sandwich.
4. Repeat with remaining bread slices, tomato slices and the filling to make three more sandwiches.
   Serve hot.

● **Eggless Mayonnaise is readily available at most provision stores.**

****

SPINACH AND CARROT RICE

Easy, colourful and tasty.

⇩

Preparation time: 10 minutes.
Cooking time: 15 minutes.
Serves 4.

⇩

2 cups cooked rice
½ teaspoon cumin seeds (jeera)
2 onions, sliced
2 large cloves garlic, chopped
²/₃ cup grated carrots
2 cups chopped spinach
1 seasoning cube (vegetarian)
2 tablespoons butter
salt and pepper to taste

1. Heat the butter and add the cumin seeds.
2. When they crackle, add the onions and garlic and sauté for 2 minutes.
3. Add the carrots and spinach and sauté for another minute.
4. Add the rice, seasoning cube, salt, pepper and ¼ cup of water and mix well.
5. Cook on a slow flame for 5 to 7 minutes till the moisture evaporates.
   Serve hot.

- ½ **cup uncooked rice makes approximately 2 cups cooked rice.**

****

CHEESE AND OATMEAL COOKIES

Picture on page 36
⇩

Nutritious whole wheat and oat cookies.
⇩

Preparation time: 5 minutes.
Cooking time: 15 minutes.
Makes 12 - 14 cookies.
⇩

½ cup butter
¼ cup cheese spread
1 teaspoon cumin seeds (jeera)
½ teaspoon black pepper, crushed
1 cup whole wheat flour (gehun ka atta)
¼ cup quick rolled oats
⇩

Other ingredients
butter for greasing

1. Cream the butter and cheese spread till light and fluffy.
2. Add the cumin seeds, black pepper, wheat flour and oats and knead gently into a soft dough.
3. Roll out the dough into a sheet of 6 mm. (¼") thickness. Prick with a fork at regular intervals.
4. Cut out 12 to 14 circles using a 50 mm. (2") cookie cutter and place them on a greased baking tray.
5. Bake in a pre-heated oven at 180ºC (360ºF) for 15 minutes or till the cookies are golden brown.
6. Remove the cookies from the oven and allow them to cool.
   Store in an air-tight container.

****

SPICY CHAPATI ROLLS

Easy to make and delicious to eat frankies.

⇩

Preparation time: 10 minutes.
Cooking time: 10 minutes.
Makes 4 rolls.

⇩

4 chapatis

⇩

For the filling
1 onion, sliced
1 large potato, peeled and grated
4 nos. baby corn, sliced
½ cup peppers, diced (red, yellow or green)
2 tablespoons roasted peanuts, crushed
½ teaspoon chilli powder
½ teaspoon garam masala
1 seasoning cube (vegetarian), optional
1 tablespoon lemon juice
1 tablespoon oil
salt to taste

For the filling
1. Heat the oil in a non-stick pan, add the onion and potato and sauté for 4 to 5 minutes.
2. Add all the other ingredients except the lemon juice and cook for further 2 minutes.
3. Remove from the fire. Add the lemon juice, mix well and keep aside.

How to proceed

1. Divide the filling into four equal portions.
2. Warm the chapatis lightly.
3. Place one portion of the filling at one side of the chapati. Roll up tightly.
4. Repeat for the remaining chapatis and filling. Serve warm with ketchup or chutney.

****

TRICOLOUR RICE

Picture on page 54
⇩
Cheesy rice topped with stir-fried vegetables.
⇩
Preparation time: 15 minutes.
Cooking time: 30 minutes.
Serves 4.
⇩

For the rice
½ cup rice
1 onion, chopped
1 clove garlic, chopped
1 teaspoon cumin seeds (jeera)
1 tablespoon butter
salt to taste
⇩
For the cheese sauce
1 teaspoon plain flour (maida)
1 teaspoon butter
¾ cup milk
2 cheese slices
salt to taste

⇩
For the stir-fried vegetables
½ cup french beans, cut into small pieces
½ cup carrots, diced
½ cup sweet corn kernels
3 teaspoons butter
salt to taste

For the rice
1. Wash and soak the rice in water for about 20 minutes. Drain and keep aside.
2. Heat the butter in a saucepan. Add the cumin seeds and when they crackle, add the onion and garlic and sauté for 2 minutes.
3. Add the rice, salt and 1 cup of hot water and simmer on a slow flame till the rice is cooked. Keep aside.

For the cheese sauce
1. Melt the butter, add the flour and cook on a slow flame for 2 minutes, while stirring throughout.
2. Add the milk gradually while stirring continuously, so that no lumps form. Bring it to a boil.
3. Add the cheese slices and salt and mix well.
4. Remove from the fire and keep aside.

For the stir-fried vegetables
1. Blanch all the vegetables separately in salted hot water.
2. Stir-fry the french beans, carrots and corn separately using 1 teaspoon of butter for each. Keep aside.

How to proceed
1. Transfer the rice onto a serving plate.
2. Reheat the cheese sauce and pour on top of the rice.
3. Arrange the stir-fried vegetables on top of the rice. Serve hot.

****

SUNKEN SUBMARINES

Submarine rolls topped with cheesy corn and vegetables.

⇩

Preparation time: 10 minutes.
Cooking time: 15 minutes.
Makes 6 rolls.

⇩

6 hot dog rolls
1 tablespoon butter
1 cup boiled vegetables
(french beans, carrots, green peas, potatoes, cauliflower)
½ cup cooked corn kernels
1 green chilli, chopped
salt and pepper to taste

⇩

For the white sauce
1 tablespoon butter
1 tablespoon plain flour (maida)
1 cup milk
salt to taste

⇩

For the topping
6 tablespoons grated cooking cheese

For the white sauce
1. Melt the butter, add the flour and cook on a slow flame for 2 minutes, while stirring throughout.
2. Add the milk gradually while stirring continuously, so that no lumps form and bring it to a boil.
3. Add salt and mix well. Remove from the fire and keep aside.

How to proceed

1. Slit each roll horizontally. Butter lightly.
2. Mix the boiled vegetables, corn, white sauce, green chilli, salt and pepper.
3. Stuff each roll with a little vegetable mixture.
4. Sprinkle the grated cheese and grill in a hot oven at 200ºC (400ºF) for 8 to 10 minutes.
   Serve hot.

****

EASY CHEESY VEGETABLE PASTA

You will never have trouble making this easy and delicious pasta.

⇩

Preparation time: 10 minutes.
Cooking time: 10 minutes.
Serves 4.

⇩

2 cups cooked pasta (macaroni or fusilli)
1 cup boiled vegetables
(carrots, peas, french beans etc.), diced
½ cup capsicum, sliced
½ cup milk
3 cheese slices
1 teaspoon butter
salt and pepper to taste

1. Heat the butter in a pan and sauté the capsicum in it for 2 minutes.
2. Add the milk and cheese slices and bring to a boil.
3. Add the vegetables, salt and pepper and mix well.

31

4. Toss the cooked pasta in the sauce and bring to a boil. Serve hot with toast or garlic bread.

● **Approximately 1¼ cups of dried pasta will yield 2 cups of cooked pasta.**

****

CORN FILLED BREAD TARTLETS

Easy to make bread tartlets filled with a cheesy corn mixture.
⇩
Preparation time: 5 minutes.
Cooking time: 15 minutes.
Makes 6 tartlets .
⇩
6 bread slices
2 teaspoons
melted butter
⇩
For the filling
2 teaspoons butter
2 teaspoons plain flour (maida)
½ cup milk
2 tablespoons grated cheese
½ cup sweet corn kernels, cooked
salt and pepper to taste
⇩
For baking
2 tablespoons grated cheese

1. Lightly grease a muffin tray or 6 tart moulds and keep aside.
2. Remove the crusts from the bread slices.

32

3. Flatten each slice using a rolling pin.
4. Press each slice of the flattened bread into the greased muffin tray or in the tart moulds.
5. Brush the bread tartlets with melted butter.
6. Bake in a pre-heated oven at 150°C (300°F) for 5 to 7 minutes.

For the filling
1. Heat the butter in a saucepan, add the flour and cook on a slow flame for 2 minutes, while stirring throughout.
2. Gradually, add the milk while stirring continuously so that no lumps form. Bring it to a boil.
3. Remove from the fire, add the cheese, corn, salt and pepper and mix well.

How to proceed
1. Spoon the filling mixture into the baked bread tartlets.
2. Sprinkle the grated cheese on top and bake in a pre-heated oven at 180°C (360°F) for 3 to 4 minutes. Serve hot.

● **You can use any other filling of your choice instead of the corn filling.**

****

CRISPY PEANUT POTATO CHAAT

A delicious after school treat.
⇩

Preparation Time: 5 minutes.
Cooking time: 20 minutes.
Serves 4.
⇩

4 large potatoes, boiled
½ cup roasted peanuts
1½ teaspoons chaat masala
1 teaspoon chilli powder
½ teaspoon turmeric powder (haldi)
1 teaspoon cumin seed (jeera) powder
½ teaspoon sugar
1 tablespoon lemon juice
3 tablespoons oil
salt to taste
⇩

1. Peel and cut the potatoes into even sized cubes.
2. Heat the oil in a non-stick pan, add the potatoes and sauté them over medium heat, stirring occasionally till they are crisp and golden brown in colour.
3. Add the peanuts and sauté for 1 to 2 minutes.
4. Add all the other ingredients and mix well. Serve hot.

● **If you want to use raw potatoes, peel and cut them into even sized pieces and deep fry them over a medium flame. Proceed as per the receipe.**

****

Top Left: Apple Lemon Fizz; *page 75*
Bottom Right: Chilli Bean Quesidillas; *page 49*

RICE NOODLES AND VEGETABLE MEDLEY

Vegetables and rice noodles in a sweet and sour tomato sauce.

⇩

Preparation time: 20 minutes.
Cooking time: 20 minutes.
Serves 6.

⇩

For the vegetable medley

1½ cups boiled vegetables (french beans, green peas,
carrots, cauliflower), diced
½ cup spring onion whites, chopped
12 mm. (½") piece ginger, grated
2 teaspoons chilli powder
2 tomatoes, chopped
¼ cup tomato ketchup
½ cup spring onion greens, chopped
2 teaspoons sugar
3 tablespoons oil
salt to taste

⇩

For the rice noodles

100 grams (½ packet) rice noodles (dried rice vermicelli)
1 teaspoon oil
salt to taste

⇩

For the garnish

1 tablespoon chopped coriander

Top Right: Delicious Sandwiches; *page 22*
Bottom Left: Cheese and Oatmeal Cookies; *page 26*

For the vegetable medley

1. Heat the oil in a saucepan and sauté the spring onion whites till they turn translucent.
2. Add the ginger and chilli powder and stir for a few more minutes.
3. Then add the tomatoes and tomato ketchup and stir again.
4. Finally, add the vegetables, spring onion greens, sugar, salt and ½ cup of water and cook for about 10 minutes. Keep aside.

For the rice noodles

1. Place the rice noodles in a large bowl.
2. In another pan, boil about 1 litre of water with the salt and oil. When it comes to a boil, pour the water over the raw rice noodles. Cover and keep aside for 10 minutes.
3. Drain and keep aside.

How to proceed

1. Place the rice noodles in a serving plate.
2. Top with the vegetable medley.
   Serve hot, garnished with the chopped coriander.

****

BUTTERY CORN ON THE COB

Tender sweet corn tossed in butter.

⇩

Preparation time: 2 minutes.
Cooking time: 20 minutes.
Makes 2 cobs.

⇩

2 sweet corn cobs
2 to 3 tablespoons butter
salt and pepper to taste

1. Steam the corn cobs till tender.
2. Using a knife, spread butter on both corn cobs.
3. Sprinkle salt and pepper and serve immediately.

● **You can use chilli powder or chaat masala instead of salt and pepper.**

****

COOKED RICE PANCAKES

A delicious recipe to use any left-over rice.

⇩

Preparation time: 10 minutes.
Cooking time: 20 minutes.
Makes 10 to 12 pancakes.

⇩

2 cups cooked rice
1/3 cup grated carrot
1/3 cup chopped spring onion
1/3 cup shredded cabbage
1/4 cup whole wheat flour (gehun ka atta)
1/2 cup Bengal gram flour (besan)
1/2 teaspoon turmeric powder (haldi)
1/4 teaspoon asafoetida (hing)
2 green chillies, finely chopped
2 tablespoons curds
2 tablespoons chopped coriander
salt to taste

⇩

Other ingredients
oil to cook

1. Combine all the ingredients except the oil in a bowl.
2. Add enough water to make a soft dough.
3. Divide the dough into 10 to 12 equal portions.
4. Using wet hands, press one portion of the dough onto a damp cloth to form a 100 mm. (4") diameter circle.
5. Lift the cloth and upturn the pancake on to a non-stick tava.
6. Cook on both sides till golden brown using a little oil.
7. Repeat with the remaining dough to make 10 to 12 pancakes.
Serve hot with green chutney, page 81

40

BAKED POTATOES

Baked jacket potatoes filled with beans, corn or cream cheese will be loved by children.

Preparation time: 10 minutes.
Cooking time: 50 minutes.
Serves 6.

6 large potatoes
oil for cooking
salt to taste

For the bean filling (for 6 potatoes)
1 small can (225 grams) baked beans
1 small onion, finely chopped
1 tablespoon oil or butter
salt and pepper to taste
4 tablespoons grated cheese for topping

For the corn filling (for 6 potatoes)
1 cup sweet corn kernels, cooked
1 small onion, finely chopped
1 green chilli, finely chopped
1 recipe white sauce, page 30
1 tablespoon butter
salt and pepper to taste
4 tablespoons grated cheese for topping

For the cream cheese filling (for 6 potatoes)
1 cup fresh thick curds
1 tablespoon fresh cream
1 green chilli, finely chopped
salt to taste

41

1. Brush the potatoes with oil. Sprinkle with salt.
2. Wrap in an aluminium foil and bake in a hot oven at 200°C (400°F) till tender (about 30 minutes).
3. Cool slightly and split each baked potato horizontally into two.
4. Scoop the potato halves a little so that a slight depression is formed for the filling.

For the bean filling
1. Heat the oil and fry the onion for 1/2 minute.
2. Add the baked beans and cook for 2 minutes.
3. Add salt and pepper.

For the corn filling
1. Heat the butter and fry the onion for 1/2 minute.
2. Add the green chilli and fry again for a few seconds.
3. Add the corn, white sauce, salt and pepper and cook for 1 minute.

For the cream cheese filling
Mix all the ingredients thoroughly and chill.

How to proceed
1. Fill each potato half with the filling of your choice (the quantities of each filling are given for six potatoes and should be adjusted as required).
2. If using cream cheese filling, serve the hot potatoes with the cold cream cheese.
3. If using the bean or corn filling, top with the grated cheese and bake in a hot oven at 200°C (400°F) for 10 minutes. Serve hot.

● **You can microwave to cook the potatoes for 7 to 10 minutes. Remember to pierce them with a fork before you microwave them. Do not use any foil to wrap the potatoes.**

****

SPINACH AND CHEESE PANCAKES

Wheat flour pancakes filled with a spinach, tomato and cheese mixture.

⇩

Preparation time: 10 minutes.
Cooking time: 20 minutes.
Makes 8 pancakes.

⇩

For the pancakes
1/3 cup whole wheat flour (gehun ka atta)
1/3 cup plain flour (maida)
1/3 cup milk
2 tablespoons melted butter
salt to taste

⇩

Other ingredients
butter or oil for cooking

⇩

For the spinach and cheese filling
2 onions, chopped
2 cloves garlic, chopped
1 cup spinach, chopped
2 large tomatoes, chopped
½ cup cheese, grated
2 teaspoons butter
salt to taste

For the pancakes

1. Mix all the ingredients with 1 cup of water to make a smooth batter.
2. Heat a 125 mm. (5") diameter non-stick pan, pour a ladleful of the batter and tilt the pan around quickly so that the batter coats the pan evenly.
3. Cook the pancake on each side for 30 seconds approximately.
4. Repeat for the remaining batter to make 8 pancakes, greasing the pan with butter, if required.

For spinach and cheese filling

1. Heat butter in a pan, add the onions and garlic and sauté for 2 minutes.
2. Add the spinach, tomatoes and salt and cook for a further
   5 minutes.
3. Remove from the fire and add the grated cheese. Mix well.

How to proceed

1. Spoon 2 tablespoons of the spinach and cheese filling into each pancake.
2. Fold each pancake into half and serve immediately.

****

PEPPY PENNE

 A super quick recipe for pasta.
⇩
Preparation time: 5 minutes.
Cooking time: 10 minutes.
Serves 4.
⇩
2 cups cooked penne (pasta)
½ cup mixed boiled vegetables
5 tablespoons instant tomato soup powder
½ cup milk
¼ cup grated cheese
⇩

1. Combine the tomato soup powder with 1 cup of water and mix well so that no lumps remain.
2. Put it into a saucepan and bring to a boil.
3. Add the milk and cheese and simmer.
4. Add the cooked penne and vegetables.
5. Toss well and serve immediately.

● **You can use your favourite flavour of soup instead of the tomato soup powder.**

****

CORN AND POTATO FRITTERS

A snack which can be made in a jiffy.

⇩

Preparation time: 10 minutes.
Cooking time: 10 minutes.
Makes 30 fritters.

⇩

1 cup potato, peeled and grated
½ cup onion, grated
½ cup sweet corn kernels, boiled
3 tablespoons chilli sauce
¼ cup whole wheat flour (gehun ka atta)
salt to taste

⇩

Other ingredients
oil for deep frying

1. Squeeze and drain the liquid from the grated potato and put it in a mixing bowl.
2. Add the remaining ingredients and mix well.
3. Heat oil in a kadhai and drop spoonfuls of the mixture into it.
4. Deep fry till golden brown. Drain on absorbent paper.
5. Serve hot with a relish of your choice.

● **You can also make patties from this mixture and shallow fry them if you like.**

****

ORIENTAL NOODLE ROSTI

Noodle pancakes topped with stir-fried vegetables.
⇩
Preparation time: 10 minutes.
Cooking time: 25 minutes.
Serves 4.
⇩
For the noodle rosti
1 packet instant noodles
1 seasoning cube (vegetarian)
salt to taste
oil for cooking

⇩
For the stir-fried vegetable topping
2 cups shredded vegetables
(carrots, french beans, cabbage, bean sprouts)
1 tablespoon oil
salt to taste
⇩
Other ingredients
1 recipe Hot and Sour Sauce, page 82

For the noodle rosti
1. Heat plenty water in a broad saucepan.
2. Cook the noodles in the boiling water for 2 minutes.
3. Drain and mix the noodles with the seasoning cube and salt.
4. Divide the noodles into four equal portions.
5. Heat a 125 mm. (5") diameter non-stick pan with 1 teaspoon of oil.
6. Loosely place one portion of the cooked noodles on the non-stick pan.
7. Cook the noodle rosti on both sides until golden brown in colour.
8. Repeat with the remaining noodles to make 3 more rostis.

For the stir-fried vegetable topping

1. Heat the oil, add the shredded vegetables and salt and cook on a high flame for 3 to 4 minutes.
2. Remove from the fire and keep aside.

How to proceed

On each serving plate, place one noodle rosti, top with a portion of the stir-fried vegetables and spoon the Hot and Sour Sauce over.

Serve immediately.

****

MASALA FRIES

Picture on page 53
⇩
An all-time favourite.
⇩
Preparation time: 10 minutes.
Cooking time: 15 minutes.
Serves 4.
⇩
4 large potatoes, peeled and cut into fingers
1 teaspoon chilli powder
½ teaspoon cumin seed (jeera) powder
¼ teaspoon black salt
salt to taste
⇩
Other ingredients
oil for deep frying
lemon wedges to serve

1. Parboil the potatoes in salted water for 5 to 7 minutes. Drain and keep aside.
2. Mix together the chilli powder, cumin seed powder, black salt and salt in a small bowl. Keep aside.
3. Deep fry the potato fingers in hot oil over a medium flame till they are crisp.
4. Drain on absorbent paper and sprinkle the masala mixture on top.
   Serve hot with lemon wedges and ketchup.

- **Use the variety of potatoes with a higher starch content popularly called French Fries Potatoes.**
- **You can use a serrated knife to make crinkled potato fingers as shown in the picture on page 53.**

****

CHILLI BEAN QUESIDILLAS

Picture on page 35
⇩
Cheese and baked beans make a great filling for quesidillas.
⇩

Preparation time: 5 minutes.
Cooking time: 20 minutes.
Serves 3.
⇩
For the tortillas
½ cup whole wheat flour (gehun ka atta)
½ cup plain flour (maida)
2 teaspoons oil
¼ teaspoon salt

49

⇓

To be mixed into a filling
¼ cup baked beans (canned)
¼ cup cooking cheese or mozzarella cheese, grated
1 tablespoon chilli sauce
1 tablespoon chopped coriander

⇓

Other ingredients
butter or oil for cooking

For the tortillas
1. Mix all the ingredients to make a soft dough by adding enough water.
2. Knead the dough well.
3. Divide into 6 portions. Roll out into thin rounds of 150 mm. (6") diameter.
4. Cook lightly on a tava (griddle) and keep aside.

How to proceed
1. Divide the filling into 3 equal portions.
2. Spread one portion of the filling on a tortilla. Cover with another tortilla.
3. Repeat with the remaining tortillas and filling to make 2 more quesidillas.
4. Heat a tava (griddle) and using a little butter, cook the prepared quesidillas on both sides until golden brown in colour.
   Serve hot with salsa or tomato ketchup.

****

SPICY SUBMARINES

Picture on page 53
⇩
A hot and spicy submarine roll with an Oriental vegetable topping
⇩
Preparation time: 5 minutes.
Cooking time: 10 minutes.
Makes 4 submarines.
⇩
4 hot dog rolls
butter for cooking
⇩

For the filling
1 cup paneer (cottage cheese), cubed
½ cup spring onions, chopped
1 cup mushrooms, sliced
½ cup peppers (red, yellow or green), sliced
1 teaspoon Schezwan sauce
4 tablespoons tomato ketchup
1 tablespoon oil
salt to taste
⇩
For the garnish
grated paneer
spring onion greens

For the filling
1. Heat the oil in a saucepan, add all the ingredients and sauté for 2 minutes.
2. Remove from the fire and keep aside.

How to proceed

1. Slit each hot dog roll horizontally. Butter and toast lightly.
2. Reheat the filling and spread a little of it and stuff each roll. Garnish with paneer and spring onion greens. Serve immediately.

● **Schezwan sauce is readily available in bottles at most grocery stores.**

****

PIZZA IN A PAN

Children's all-time favourite recipe made within minutes on a tava (griddle).

⇩

Preparation time: 30 minutes.
Cooking time: 45 minutes.
Makes 2 pizzas.

⇩

For the pizza base

2 cups plain flour (maida)
2 teaspoons (10 grams) fresh yeast, crumbled
1 teaspoon sugar
1 teaspoon salt
1 tablespoon oil

Top Left: Masala Fries; *page 48*
Bottom Right: Spicy Submarines; *page 51*

⇩

For the tomato sauce
4 large tomatoes
1 small onion, chopped
1 teaspoon garlic, chopped
¼ cup tomato ketchup
1 teaspoon sugar
½ teaspoon dried oregano
2 tablespoons oil
salt to taste

⇩

For the topping
½ cup spring onions, chopped
½ cup mushrooms, sliced
1 cup cooking cheese or mozzarella cheese, grated

⇩

Other ingredients
1 tablespoon oil for cooking

For pizza base
1. Combine all the ingredients except the oil in a bowl and knead into a soft dough using enough water until it is smooth and elastic.
2. Add the oil and knead again.
3. Cover the dough with a wet muslin cloth and allow it to prove till it doubles in volume (approx 15 to 20 minutes).
4. Press the dough lightly to remove the air.
5. Divide the dough into 2 equal parts.
6. Roll out each portion into a circle of 250 mm. (10") diameter and 6 mm. (¼") thickness.

Top Right: Chatpata Chaat; *page 23*
Bottom Right: Tricolour Rice; *page 28*

For the tomato sauce

1. Blanch the tomatoes in boiling water.
2. Peel, cut into quarters and deseed the tomatoes.
3. Chop finely and keep the tomato pulp aside.
4. Heat the oil, add the onion and garlic and sauté for a few minutes.
5. Add the tomato pulp and allow it to simmer for 10 to 15 minutes until the sauce reduces a little.
6. Add the ketchup, sugar and salt and simmer for some more time.
7. Finally, add the oregano and mix well.

How to proceed

1. Heat half the oil in a non-stick pan and place a pizza base on it.
2. Spread half the tomato sauce over the pizza base.
3. Top with half the spring onions, mushrooms and cheese.
4. Cover the pan with a lid and cook on a very slow flame for 10 to 12 minutes or till the base is evenly browned.
5. Repeat with the remaining ingredients to make another pizza.

● **The trick in making this pizza is to keep the flame sufficiently low so that the base does not burn while cooking.**

****

SWEET TREATS

GRANOLA BARS

Picture on page 64
⇩
A power packed breakfast bar that can be taken to school.
⇩

Preparation time: 5 minutes.
Cooking time: 15 minutes.
Makes 16 pieces.
⇩

¾ cup crushed cornflakes
¾ cup quick rolled oats
½ cup mixed nuts (almonds, pistachios, walnuts,
cashewnuts), chopped
2 tablespoons melon seeds (charmagaz)
1 tablespoon sultanas
1 cup sugar
oil to grease

1. Lightly roast the oats, nuts and melon seeds and keep aside to cool.
2. When cooled, mix together the cornflakes, toasted oats, melon seeds, nuts and sultanas.
3. In a heavy bottomed pan, add the sugar and melt it over gentle heat, stirring continuously till the sugar is light brown in colour (caramelised).
4. Remove from the fire, add the rest of the ingredients and mix well.
5. Pour this mixture onto a greased marble or stone surface.

6. Using a large greased rolling pin, roll it out lightly to form a square approximately 200 mm. x 200 mm. (8" x 8").
7. While it is still warm, cut out rectangular bars of 25 mm. x 100 mm. (1" x 4").
   Store in an air-tight container.

- **Sugar burns very quickly, so give it your full attention.**
- **Grease your hands, the marble top and the rolling pin generously with oil. This will prevent the bars from sticking and also prevent your hands from getting burnt.**
- **Remove the sugar from the flame just when it starts to caramelise because it continues to brown even after it is removed from heat.**

****

WALNUT BUTTERSCOTCH BARS

A butter cookie base topped with a walnut butterscotch mixture, baked till crisp and chewy.

⇩

Preparation time: 10 minutes.
Cooking time: 30 minutes.
Makes 18 bars.

⇩

For the crust
½ cup butter
3 tablespoons castor sugar
1½ cups plain flour (maida)

⇩

For the topping
½ cup castor sugar
½ cup chopped walnuts
¼ cup butter
¼ cup cream
¼ cup honey
½ teaspoon vanilla essence.

For the crust
1. Cream the butter and castor sugar in a bowl till light and fluffy.
2. Add the flour and knead gently into a soft dough, using cold water only if required.
3. Roll out into a large sheet and put in a 150 mm. x 200 mm. (6" x 8") baking tray.
4. Refrigerate for 15 minutes or till firm.
5. Prick the pastry with a fork at regular intervals and bake in a pre-heated oven at 180°C (360°F) for 10 minutes.
6. Remove from the oven and keep aside.

For the topping

Combine all the ingredients in a saucepan and cook over gentle heat for 4 to 5 minutes.

How to proceed

1. Pour the topping mixture over the half baked crust and spread it evenly over the surface.
2. Bake in a pre-heated oven at 200°C (400°F) for 20 minutes or till the topping is golden brown in colour. Remove from the oven.
3. While it is still warm, cut into rectangular bars of 25 mm. x 60 mm. (1" x 2½") .
4. Cool completely and store in an air-tight container.

****

FRUIT AND JELLY CUPS

Picture on page 63
⇩
An attractively presented fruit salad.
⇩
Preparation time: 10 minutes.
Cooking time: 5 minutes.
Makes 4 cups.
⇩

For the fruit cups
2 apples
1 teaspoon lemon juice

⇩
For the fruit salad
1 apple, diced
1 mango, peeled and diced
1 banana, sliced
10 to 12 cherries
¼ cup black grapes
1 teaspoon chaat masala
⇩
Other ingredients
1 packet strawberry jelly (vegetarian)

Make the strawberry jelly, as per the directions on the packet and refrigerate till it sets .

For the fruit cups
1. Cut the apples into two halves.
2. Scoop out the centres to make 4 apple cups.
3. Apply the lemon juice and keep aside.

How to proceed
1. Mix the apple, mango, banana, cherries, black grapes and chaat masala together and refrigerate.
2. For serving, fill the fruit mixture into the apple cups.
3. Cut the jelly into small squares and decorate the fruit cups.
   Serve chilled.

● **You can cut the jelly onto attractive shapes using cookie cutters.**

****

€ASY CHOCOLATE
MOUSSE

A delicious, no fuss dessert your kids are sure to love.

⇩

Preparation time: 10 minutes.
Cooking time: 5 minutes.
Serves 4.

⇩

2 cups (250 grams) dark chocolate, finely chopped
1½ tablespoons golden syrup
1 cup (200 grams) fresh cream

⇩

To garnish
2 crushed sweet biscuits
½ cup chopped mixed fruits

1. Combine the chocolate, golden syrup and 1½ tablespoons of water in a saucepan and melt over gentle heat till it is a smooth mixture. Cool slightly.
2. Whip the cream till soft peaks form and fold in the chocolate mixture.
3. Pour this into 4 cups.
4. Refrigerate for 4 to 6 hours or till the mousse has set.
5. Serve chilled garnished with crushed biscuits and chopped fruit.

* *

Top Right: Mango Ice-cream; *page 72*
Strawberry Ice-cream; *page 73*
Bottom Left: Fruit and Jelly Cups; *page 60*

ALMOND PISTACHIO PRALINE TRIANGLES

Picture on facing page
⇩

A delicious praline made of nuts and poppy seeds. A great snack for any time of the day.
⇩

Preparation time: 10 minutes.
Cooking time: 15 minutes.
Serves 4.
⇩

1/3 cup coarsely powdered nuts (almonds and pistachio)
2 tablespoons melon seeds (charmagaz)
2 tablespoons poppy seeds (khus khus)
1/4 teaspoon cardamom (elaichi) powder
1/2 cup sugar
oil to grease

1. In a heavy bottomed pan, add the sugar and melt it over gentle heat, stirring continuously till the sugar is light brown in colour (caramelised).
2. Remove from the fire, add the rest of the ingredients and mix well.
3. Pour this mixture onto a greased marble or stone surface.

Top Right: Granola Bars; *page 57*
Centre: Speckled Bubble Bars; *page 70*
Bottom Left: Almond Pistachio Praline Triangles; *recipe above*

4. Using a large greased rolling pin, roll out the praline as thinly as you can.
5. While it is still warm, cut into triangles. Allow it to cool completely.
6. Store in an air-tight container.

- **Sugar burns very quickly, so give it your full attention.**
- **Remove the sugar from the flame just when it starts to caramelise because it continues to brown even after it is removed from heat.**

****

JAM TREATS

A healthier alternative to the traditional jam tarts using whole wheat pastry.

⇩

Preparation time: 10 minutes.
Cooking time: 30 minutes.
Makes 9.

⇩

1½ cups whole wheat flour (gehun ka atta)
½ cup butter
¹/₃ cup castor sugar

⇩

Other ingredients
4 to 5 tablespoons of your favourite jam

1. In a bowl, combine the flour, butter and sugar and rub using your fingertips till it resembles bread crumbs.
2. Knead gently into a soft dough, using cold water only if required.
3. Roll out into a rectangle of 150 mm. x 187 mm. (6" x 7½") and 6 mm. (¼") thick.

4. Cut into 3 equal strips lengthwise.
5. Place these on a baking tray.
6. Using your fingertips, create a cavity in the centre of each strip.
7. Spoon some jam into each cavity.
8. Decorate the jam treats using strips of left over pastry.
9. Bake in a pre-heated oven at 180°C (360°F) for 20 to 30 minutes till golden brown.
10. Cut each strip into 3 equal parts.
11. Cool and store in an air-tight container.

****

ORANGE RAISIN MUFFINS

Picture on page 18
⇩
Children will love these any time of the day.
⇩
Preparation time: 10 minutes.
Cooking time: 20 minutes.
Makes 10 muffins.
⇩
1 cup plain flour (maida)
¼ teaspoon soda bi-carbonate
½ cup butter
1 tablespoon orange squash
1 teaspoon orange rind, grated (optional)
¹/₃ cup castor sugar
½ cup condensed milk
¼ cup raisins
¹/₃ cup cream

1. Sieve the flour with the soda bi-carb. Keep aside.
2. Cream the butter, orange squash, orange rind and sugar till smooth and creamy.
3. Add the condensed milk, raisins, cream and flour and mix well.
4. Spoon the mixture into 10 greased and dusted muffin moulds.
5. Bake in a pre-heated oven at 180°C (360°F) for 15 to 20 minutes or until a skewer inserted in a muffin comes out clean.
6. Cool slightly and unmould.

- **You can line the muffin moulds with paper cups insted of greasing the moulds. This way they do not crumble when unmoulding.**

****

PIÑA COLADA DOUGHNUTS

Delightful doughnuts filled with pineapple, coconut and sultanas.

⇩

Preparation time: 20 minutes.
Cooking time: 15 minutes.
Makes 10.

⇩

For the dough
1½ cups plain flour (maida)
2 teaspoons (10 grams) fresh yeast, crumbled
3 tablespoons sugar
2 tablespoons cream (optional)
1 teaspoon oil
a pinch salt

⇩

To be mixed into a filling
1 slice pineapple, chopped
2 tablespoons grated coconut
2 tablespoons sultanas
2 tablespoons brown sugar
¼ teaspoon cinnamon powder

⇩

Other ingredients
oil to deep fry

For the dough
1. Combine all the ingredients except the oil in a bowl and knead into a soft dough using enough water until it is smooth and elastic.
2. Add the oil and knead again.
3. Cover with a damp muslin cloth and allow it to prove till it is double in volume (approx. 15 to 20 minutes).
4. Press the dough lightly with your palms to remove the air.
5. Roll out the dough into a 5 mm. thick sheet.
6. Using a 75 mm. (3") cookie cutter, cut out 10 circles.

How to proceed
1. Place a spoonful of the filling mixture on each of the 5 dough circles.
2. Place the other 5 dough circles on top of the filling mixture and seal the edges tightly.
3. Deep fry these doughnuts in hot oil over a medium flame till golden brown on both sides.
Serve hot.

****

SPECKLED BUBBLE BARS

Picture on page 64
⇩
Sesame and puffed rice bars.
⇩
Preparation time: 5 minutes.
Cooking time: 10 minutes.
Makes 6 bars.
⇩

¹/₃ cup grated jaggery (gur)
1 cup puffed rice (mamra), toasted
¼ cup sesame seeds (til), toasted
a pinch cardamom powder
oil for greasing

1. Melt the jaggery in a heavy bottomed pan, on a slow flame until it caramelises.
2. Remove from the fire and add in the rest of the ingredients. Mix well.
3. Pour this mixture onto a greased marble or stone surface.
4. Using a large greased rolling pin, roll out the praline to a 150 mm. x 112 mm. (6" x 4½ ") rectangle and 12 mm. (½") thickness.
5. Cut into 75 mm. X 27 mm. (3" X 1½") bars.
   Store in an air-tight container.

● **To test when the jaggery is caramelised, drop a little of the melted jaggery into ice cold water. If it turns hard and brittle, it is ready to be removed from the flame.**

****

SUPER SNACK BARS

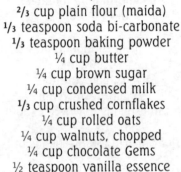

Serve these with milk.
⇩
Preparation time: 10 minutes.
Cooking time: 40 minutes.
Makes 12 bars.
⇩
$2/3$ cup plain flour (maida)
$1/3$ teaspoon soda bi-carbonate
$1/3$ teaspoon baking powder
¼ cup butter
¼ cup brown sugar
¼ cup condensed milk
$1/3$ cup crushed cornflakes
¼ cup rolled oats
¼ cup walnuts, chopped
¼ cup chocolate Gems
½ teaspoon vanilla essence
a pinch salt

1. Sieve the flour with the soda bi-carbonate and baking powder. Keep aside.
2. Cream the butter and brown sugar till light and fluffy.
3. Add all the other ingredients and mix well.
4. Press this mixture into a greased 150 mm. x 150 mm. (6" x 6") baking tray.
5. Bake in a pre-heated oven at 180°C (360°F) for 30 to 40 minutes till the crust is golden brown.
6. Cut into rectangles of 25 mm. x 75 mm. (1" x 3") while it is still hot.
7. Cool completely and store in an air-tight container.

- **You can also use granulated sugar instead of brown sugar.**

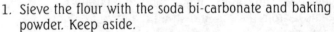

MANGO ICE-CREAM

Picture on page 63
⇩
A delicious fresh fruit ice-cream.
⇩
Preparation time: 10 minutes.
Cooking time: 5 minutes.
Makes 4 scoops.
⇩

½ cup fresh mango purée
½ cup milk
1 teaspoon cornflour
⅓ cup fresh cream
4 tablespoons powdered sugar

1. Mix the cornflour in 1 to 2 tablespoons of cold water and keep aside.
2. Heat the milk in a heavy bottomed pan. When it comes to a boil, add the dissolved cornflour, 2 tablespoons of powdered sugar and simmer for 3 to 4 minutes.
3. Remove from the fire and strain the mixture. Cool completely.
4. Whip the cream with the remaining powdered sugar till soft peaks form.
5. Mix the cooled milk mixture with the cream and mango purée.
6. Pour into a shallow freezeproof dish and freeze till slushy.
7. Remove from the freezer and beat till smooth and creamy.
8. Freeze again until firm.

STRAWBERRY ICE-CREAM Picture on page 63
Use ⅓ cup strawberry purée instead of mango purée for the
above recipe.
You will need to increase the quantity of sugar.

****

YOGHURT LOLLIES

*Fruit and yoghurt frozen to make a healthy ice-cream your
kids are sure to love.*

Preparation time: 5 minutes.
No cooking.
Makes 6.

1 cup fresh curds
¾ cup fruit purée (mango, strawberry)
3 to 4 tablespoons sugar
½ teaspoon vanilla essence

1. Combine all the ingredients in a liquidizer and blend to a
   smooth mixture.
2. Pour into plastic lolly moulds and freeze for 6 to 8 hours
   till they are firm.
3. Insert wooden ice-cream sticks into the frozen lollies and
   unmould.
   Serve immediately.

Variation:
CHOCOLATE YOGHURT LOLLIES Use ½ recipe of Chocolate
Truffle Sauce (page 83) instead of the fruit
purée for the above recipe.

● **You can use kulfi moulds instead of lolly moulds
for freezing the lollies.**

****

DRINKS

APPLE LEMON FIZZ

Picture on page 35

A refreshing after-school drink. Makes a great punch for parties too!
⇩

Preparation time: 5 minutes.
No cooking.
Makes 2 glasses.
⇩

1 cup (200 ml.) apple juice
1 bottle (200 ml.) lemonade
2 tablespoons finely chopped cucumber
2 tablespoons finely chopped apple (optional)
1 teaspoon mint leaves, finely chopped
1 teaspoon honey

Combine all the ingredients, pour into 2 glasses and serve immediately.

● **Chill the apple juice and lemonade before mixing this drink since adding ice cubes will dilute the drink.**

****

PEACH DREAM

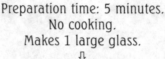

A tropical smoothie.
⇩
Preparation time: 5 minutes.
No cooking.
Makes 1 large glass.
⇩
2 tablespoons peach crush
1 tablespoon orange squash
1 cup milk, chilled
1 scoop vanilla ice-cream
⇩
For the garnish
1 teaspoon grated chocolate

1. Combine all the ingredients and blend in a liquidizer until smooth.
2. Pour into a tall glass and serve garnished with grated chocolate.

● **You can also use peach halves (canned) instead of peach crush for the above recipe.**

****

BANANA YOGHURT SHAKE

A fruity variation of the traditional lassi.

⇩

Preparation time: 5 minutes.
No cooking.
Makes 2 glasses.

⇩

1 cup fresh curds
3 tablespoons sugar
1 ripe banana, mashed
1 cup milk
½ teaspoon vanilla essence
a pinch grated nutmeg (optional)

1. Combine all the ingredients and blend in a liquidizer till smooth.
2. Pour into 2 glasses and serve immediately.

● **Use chilled curds and milk for this recipe.**

****

CHOCOLADA SHAKE

A chocolaty variation of the famous pina-colada.

⇩

Preparation time: 5 minutes.
No cooking.
Make 2 glasses.

⇩

¼ cup Chocolate Truffle Sauce, page 83
2 cups milk
¼ cup coconut cream
1 slice pineapple, chopped
2 tablespoons sugar

1. Combine all the ingredients and blend in a liquidiser till frothy.
2. Pour into 2 glasses.
   Serve chilled.

****

CHUTNEYS AND RELISHES

SWEET AND SOUR TOMATO RELISH

Picture on page 17
⇩
Preparation time: 10 minutes.
Cooking time: 25 minutes.
Makes 1 cup.
⇩

3 tomatoes, blanched and peeled
¾ cup sugar
2 tablespoons carrot, finely chopped
4 cloves garlic, peeled
4 to 5 peppercorns
1 teaspoon onion seeds (kalonji)
1 teaspoon chilli powder
1 tablespoon vinegar
salt to taste

1. Cut the tomatoes into two halves, remove the seeds and strain the juice.
2. Roughly chop the tomato pulp. Separately keep aside the tomato pulp and tomato juice.
3. In a heavy bottomed pan, add the tomato juice and sugar. Cook on a slow flame till the sugar dissolves.
4. Add the tomato pulp, carrot, garlic and peppercorns and cook on a slow flame for about 20 to 25 minutes.

5. Remove from the fire, add the kalonji, chilli powder, vinegar and salt.
6. Allow to cool and store in a refrigerator.
   Serve with chapatis or parathas.

****

CUCUMBER RELISH

A tangy cucumber relish which can be served with almost anything.

⇩

Preparation time: 10 minutes.
No cooking.
Makes 1 cup.

⇩

1 medium cucumber, peeled and chopped finely
1 small tomato, blanched, peeled and chopped finely
1 small red chilli, finely chopped
1 tablespoon vinegar
1½ tablespoons castor sugar
salt to taste

1. Combine the cucumber, tomato, red chilli, vinegar, castor sugar and salt in a bowl and mix well.
2. Keep aside for at least 2 hours before serving.

● **Make the relish a day in advance as the flavours mellow down and blend well.**

****

SWEET CHUTNEY

Preparation time: 10 minutes.
Cooking time: 5 minutes.
Makes ½ cup.
⇩

½ cup dates (khajur), chopped
1 tablespoon tamarind (imli)
¼ teaspoon chilli powder
¼ teaspoon roasted cumin seed (jeera) powder
salt to taste
⇩

1. Deseed the dates and tamarind. Wash, add ¼ cup of water
   and cook for 5 minutes. Thereafter, blend in a liquidiser and
   strain.
2. Add the chilli powder, cumin seed powder and salt. Mix well.
   Use as required.

****

GREEN CHUTNEY

Preparation time: 5 minutes.
No cooking.
Makes ¼ cup.
⇩

½ cup chopped coriander
1 green chilli, chopped
½ teaspoon lemon juice
1 teaspoon sugar
salt to taste

Put all the ingredients in a food processor and grind into a
paste, adding a little water if necessary.

****

BASIC RECIPES

HOT AND SOUR SAUCE

So easy and yet so tasty.

⇩

Preparation time: 5 minutes.
Cooking time: 10 minutes.
Makes 1 cup.

⇩

¼ cup tomato purée
½ cup vinegar
½ cup sugar
1 tablespoon chilli sauce
1 tablespoon cornflour
salt and pepper to taste

1. Mix together all the ingredients with ½ cup of water and bring to a boil.
2. Simmer for 2 to 3 minutes.
3. Cool and use as a spread or serve hot with noodles and vegetables.

- **This makes a delicious spread for frankies and cheese sandwiches.**

****

CHOCOLATE TRUFFLE SAUCE

A delicious topping for desserts.

⇩

Preparation time: 5 minutes.
Cooking time: 5 minutes.
Makes 1½ cups.

⇩

1 cup (125 grams) grated dark chocolate
½ cup milk

1. Heat the milk in a heavy bottomed pan.
2. Bring to a boil, remove from the fire and add the chocolate.
3. Mix well to get a smooth sauce.
4. Cool and use as required.

● **Chocolate truffle sauce can be made in advance and stored refrigerated.**

****

EGGLESS MAYONNAISE

Preparation time: a few minutes.
No cooking.
Makes about 1¼ teacups.
⇩

½ can (400 grams for full can) condensed milk
4 tablespoons salad oil
4 tablespoons white vinegar or lemon juice
½ teaspoon salt
1 teaspoon mustard powder
½ teaspoon pepper powder

⇩

1. Gradually mix all the ingredients together using a whisk.
   Store in a refrigerator.
2. Use as required.

****